CHAPTER 1

AND MOST CERTAINLY, THOU** (O MUHUMMED) **ART OF MOST SUBLIME AND EXALTED CHARACTER.

وَإِنَّكَ لَعَلَىٰ خُلُقٍ عَظِيمٍ ○

Holy Qur'an 68:4 [1]

HOW THE TOPIC AROSE

About ten years ago, a distant cousin of mine — Mr. Mohamed Mehtar (Farooki) [2] gave me a typed quotation by the French historian, Lamartine. The quotation [3] purported to prove that Muhummed (pbuh), the prophet of Islam, was the greatest man that ever lived. Mr. Mehtar was in the habit of passing information on to me, believing that I might put the same to some good use at the proper time and place. Before this he had presented me with **"The Call of the Minaret"** an expensive book written by (Bishop Kenneth Cragg). By analysing this book I discovered the masterful deceit of the Christian orientalists.

---

1. I urge my Muslim brethren to memorize the verse in Arabic and its meaning.
2. Mr. Mehtar was for a long time editor of the Muslim newspaper **"The Indian Views,"** in South Africa.
3. A detailed exposition of the quotation will be found on page 38.

Lamartine's tribute to our prophet inspired me and I had a great desire to share his thoughts about our ***Nabee*** with my Muslim brethren. The opportunity to do so was not long in coming.

I received a phone call from the Muslim community in Dannhauser, a small town in Northern Natal, who were organising a birthday celebration of the Holy Prophet. They invited me to give a lecture on that auspicious occasion. So I deemed it an honour and a privilege, I readily agreed. When they inquired, in view of their advertising needs, as to the subject of my lecture, I suggested on the inspiration from Lamartine, **"Muhummed (pbuh) the Greatest."**

REPEATED LET-DOWNS

On my arrival in Dannhauser, I noticed a lot of posters advertising the meeting which in essence said that Deedat would be lecturing on the subject "MUHUMMED THE GREAT." I was somewhat disheartened and, on inquiring was told that the change in the title was due to a printer's error.

Some two months later, I got another, similar invitation. This time from the Muslim community of Pretoria the administrative capital of South Africa. The subject I had mooted was the same — **"Muhummed (pbuh) the Greatest."** To my dismay the topic was again changed to "MUHUMMED THE GREAT." Identical reasons and excuses were given. Both these incidences happened in South Africa, my own country. But, let me give you one more example of our inferiority complex — so much part of the sickness of the ***Ummah.***

USA NO DIFFERENT

On my lecture tour of the mighty United States in 1977, I discovered that our soldiers in the New World also had feet of clay. Out of the many sad experiences I have had, I think that this one will suffice to prove the point.

The Muslims of Indianapolis were advised to organise a lecture for me on the subject **"What the Bible says about Muhummed (pbuh)".**[1] They agreed to advertise just that, but their timidity did not permit them to do so. They thought the topic was too provocative, so they, in their wisdom (?), toned it down to "A PROPHET IN THE BIBLE." A lifeless, insipid title you will no doubt agree. Which Hindu, Muslim, Christian or Jew would be intrigued to attend? What does **"A PROPHET"** mean? To most A PROPHET means ANY PROPHET, and who would be interested in attending a meeting where just any prophet in the Bible was debated? Job, Joel, Jonah, Ezra, Elisha, Ezekiel are just a few of the many mentioned in the Bible. As was to be expected the attendance left much to be desired.

INFERIORITY COMPLEX

What is the cause of this sickness? This inferiority complex? **"Yes!"** We are an emasculated people. Dynamism has been wringed out of us, not only by our enemies but by our own spiritless friends. We even dare not repeat Allah's Own testimony regarding his beloved —

> *And Most Certainly,*
> *Thou* (O MUHUMMED)
> *Art of most sublime*
> *And Exalted Character.* Holy Qur'an 68:4 [2]

THE MOST INFLUENTIAL

Normally, it is quite, natural for anyone to love, praise, idolize or hero-worship ones leader, be it a guru, saint or prophet: and very often we do.

---

1. A book with the same title is available absolutely **FREE** from the IPCI.
2. This verse, together with its Arabic text heads this chapter; memorize the verse with its meaning.

However, if I were to reproduce here[1] what great Muslims have said or written about our illustrious prophet, it could be played down as exaggeration, fancy or idolization by the sceptics and the opponents of Islam. Therefore, allow me to quote unbiased historians, friendly critics and even avowed enemies of that mighty Messenger of God — Muhummed (pbuh). If the tributes of the non-Muslims do not touch your hearts, then you are in the wrong faith. Opt out of Islam! There is already too much deadwood on the "ship" of Islam.

In recent times, a book has been published in America titled **"The 100,"** or the Top One Hundred, or the Greatest Hundred in History. A certain Michael H. Hart, described as a historian, mathematician and astronomer has written this novel book. He has searched history, seeking for men who had the greatest influence on mankind. In this book he gives us The hundred most influential men, including Asoka, Aristotle, Buddha, Confucius, Hitler, Plato, and Zoroaster. He does not give us a mere chart of the topmost **"one hundred"** from the point of view of their influence on people, but he evaluates the degree of their influence and rates them in order of their excellence from No. 1, through to No. 100. He gives us his reasons for the placing of his candidates. We are not asked to agree with him, but we cannot help admire the man's research and honesty.

The most amazing thing about his selection is that he has put our ***Nabee-e-Kareem,*** the Holy Prophet Muhummed (pbuh) as No. 1,[2] the first of his "100!" Thus confirming, unknowingly, God's Own testimony in His Final Revelation to the World:

---

1. For an example, see Appendix "A" at the end of this book.

2. With the kind permission of Mr. Hart, we have just reproduced the whole chapter on Muhummed (pbuh) from the **"Top 100"**. Get your **FREE** copy now from the I.P.C.I.

***MOST CERTAINLY, YOU HAVE IN THE MESSENGER OF ALLAH [1] AN EXCELLENT PATTERN** (OF BEHAVIOUR)*

لَقَدْ كَانَ لَكُمْ فِي رَسُولِ اللَّهِ أُسْوَةٌ حَسَنَةٌ

Holy Qur'an 33:21

JESUS (PBUH) No. 3!

Hart placing the Prophet of Islam as No. 1, has naturally pleased the Muslims. But his choice has shocked the Non-Muslims, more specially the Jews and the Christians, who consider this as an afront. What? Jesus (pbuh) No. 3 and Moses (pbuh) No. 40! This is for them very difficult to stomach, but what says Hart? Let us hear his arguments —

> SINCE THERE ARE ROUGHLY TWICE [2] AS MANY CHRISTIANS IN THE WORLD, IT MAY INITIALLY SEEM STRANGE THAT MUHAMMAD HAS BEEN RANKED HIGHER THAN JESUS.
>
> THERE ARE TWO PRINCIPAL REASONS FOR THAT DECISION.
>
> **FIRST**, MUHUMMAD PLAYED A FAR MORE IMPORTANT ROLE IN THE DEVELOPMENT OF ISLAM THAN JESUS DID IN THE DEVELOPMENT OF CHRISTIANITY.
>
> ALTHOUGH JESUS WAS RESPONSIBLE FOR THE MAIN ETHICAL AND MORAL PRECEPTS OF CHRISTIANITY (INSOFAR AS THESE DIFFERED FROM JUDAISM), ST. PAUL WAS THE MAIN DEVELOPER OF CHRISTIAN THEOLOGY, ITS PRINCIPAL

---

1. ***Allah:*** A proper noun for God Almighty in the Semitic languages; i.e. in the languages of Moses, Jesus and Muhummed (Peace be on them all). For more details obtain **"What is His name?"** from the I.P.C.I.

2. The latest estimate is that there are one thousand million Muslims in the world and one thousand two hundred million Christians.

PROSELYTIZER, AND THE AUTHOR OF A LARGE PORTION OF THE NEW TESTAMENT.

MUHAMMAD, HOWEVER, WAS RESPONSIBLE FOR BOTH THE THEOLOGY OF ISLAM AND ITS MAIN ETHICAL AND MORAL PRINCIPLES.

IN ADDITION, HE PLAYED THE KEY ROLE IN PROSELYTIZING THE NEW FAITH, AND IN ESTABLISHING THE RELIGIOUS PRACTICES OF ISLAM.

Michael H. Hart in his book — ***"THE 100"*** pages 38/39

PAUL THE FOUNDER OF CHRISTIANITY

According to Hart, the honour for founding Christianity is to be shared between Jesus (pbuh) and St. Paul. The latter he believes to be the real founder of Christianity.

I cannot help agreeing with Hart. Out of the total of 27 Books of the New Testament, more than half is authored by Paul. As opposed to Paul, the Master has not written a single word of the twenty-seven books. If you can lay your hands on what is called **"A Red Letter Bible,"** you will find every word alleged to have been uttered by Jesus (pbuh) — in red ink and the rest in normal black ink. Don't be shocked to find that in this so called ***"Injeel,"*** the Gospel of Jesus, over ninety percent of the 27 Books of the New Testament is printed in black ink!

This is the candid Christian confession on what they call the ***"Injeel."*** In actual any confrontation with Christian missionaries, you will find them quoting one hundred percent from Paul.

NO ONE FOLLOWS JESUS (PBUH)

Jesus (pbuh) said,

"If you love me, keep my commandments"
(John 14:15)

He said further,

> *Whosoever therefore shall break one of these least commandments, and shall teach men so, he shall be called the least in the kingdom of heaven . . ."*
>
> (Matthew 5:19)

Every Christian controversialist you question, "Do you keep the laws and the commandments?" will answer, **"No!"** if you ask further, "Why don't you?" he will if he is a Bible-thumper, invariably reply, **"The law is nailed to the cross!"** Meaning the law is done away with. **"We are now living under grace!"**

Every time you prod him with what his Lord and Master (pbuh) had said, he will confront you with something from Corinthians, Galatians, Ephesians, Philippians, etc. If you ask, "Who are they?" You will hear, "Paul, Paul, Paul!" "Who is your master?" you question, and he will say, "Jesus!" But he will ever and anon contradicts his own Jesus (pbuh) by his Paul!

No learned Christian will ever dispute the fact that the real founder of Christianity is St. Paul. Therefore, Michael H. Hart to be fair, had to place Jesus (pbuh), in slot number three.

WHY PROVOKE YOUR CUSTOMER?

This placing of Christ in the number three spot by Michael H. Hart poses a very serious question for us. Why would an American publish a book of 572 pages in America and selling in America for $15 each, go out of his way to provoke his potential readers?

Who will buy his books? Surely, not the Pakistanis and the Bangladeshis, neither the Arabs nor the Turks! Except for a few copies here and there, the overwhelming number of his customers will be from the 250 million Christians and the 6 million Jews of America. Then why did he provoke his customers? Did he not hear the dictum — **"the customer is always right!"** Of course he did. Then why his daring choice. But before I close this episode of Hart, I will allow him to make his one last apology for his "temerity.'

> "MY CHOICE OF MUHAMMAD TO LEAD THE LIST OF THE WORLD'S MOST INFLUENTIAL PERSONS MAY SURPRISE SOME READERS AND MAY BE QUESTIONED BY OTHERS, BUT HE WAS THE ONLY MAN IN HISTORY WHO WAS SUPREMELY SUCCESSFUL ON BOTH THE RELIGIOUS AND SECULAR LEVEL."
>
> Michael H. Hart

"The 100: A Ranking of the Most Influential Persons in History", New York: Hart Publishing Company, Inc., 1978, p.33.

WHO WERE HISTORY'S GREAT LEADERS

TIME, JULY 15, 1974

The world famous **"Time"**[1] carried the above rubic on its front cover. Inside the magazine were numerous essays as to **'What makes a great leader?' 'Throughout history, who qualifies?'** TIME asked a variety of historians, writers, military men, businessmen and others for their selections. Each gave his candidate according to his "light" as objectively as is humanly possible, depending on one's own awareness and prejudice.

WHO KNOWS DR. SALAZAR?

It is my habit and pleasurable duty to take non-Muslims

1. **"Time"** We are at loggerheads with this magazine. Believe it or not; they have spurned our paid advertisement as shown on page 64. The words **"FUTURE WORLD CONSTITUTION"** was referred back to us in their correspondence as "The Future World **CONFRONTATION."**

on a guided tour[1] of the largest mosque in the Southern Hemisphere — ***"The Jumma Musjid",*** Durban.

On one occasion I was hosting a Portuguese couple, a husband and wife team. At some stage during the discussion the Portuguese gentleman said that **"Dr. Salazar was the greatest man in the world!"** I did not debate the point with him as I personally knew little about Dr. Salazar except that he was a one time dictator of Portugal albeit to many a great benefactor to his nation. My poor visitor was, however, speaking according to his own knowledge, point of view and prejudice.

MUHUMMED (PBUH) CANNOT BE IGNORED!

Among the contributors to the **"Time,"** it seems that none could ignore Muhummed (pbuh).

WILLIAM McNEILL, a United States historian, of the University of Chicago, records:

> "IF YOU MEASURE LEADERSHIP BY IMPACT, THEN YOU WOULD HAVE TO NAME JESUS, BUDDHA, MOHAMMED, CONFUCIUS, THE GREAT PROPHETS OF THE WORLD . . ."

McNeill does not go into details, nor does he give us any explanation as to why he placed Jesus (pbuh) first and Muhummed (pbuh) number three. Perhaps it was by force of habit. It is very likely that McNeill is a Christian. However, we will not argue with him. Then comes —

JAMES GAVIN, described as a United States army man, a retired lieutenant general. He says —

---

1. Obtain the Video Tape — **"NON-MUSLIMS IN YOUR MOSQUE,"** available on Pal and NTSC systems from the IPCI

"AMONG LEADERS WHO HAVE MADE THE GREATEST IMPACT THROUGH AGES, I WOULD CONSIDER MOHAMMED, JESUS CHRIST, MAYBE LENIN, POSSIBLY MAO. AS FOR A LEADER WHOSE QUALITIES WE COULD MOST USE NOW, I WOULD CHOOSE JOHN F. KENNEDY."

The General does not say much more, yet we have to salute him. It calls for tremendous fortitude to pen the name Muhummed before that of Christ (peace be upon them both). It surely, was no slip of the pen.

JULES MASSERMAN, United States psychoanalyst and professor ot tne Chicago University, gives us, unlike the other contributors, the basis for making his selection. He gives us his reason for choosing his greatest LEADER of all times.

He wants us to find out, what we are really looking for in the man, the qualities that sets him apart. We may be looking for any sets of qualities. As in the case of Michael H. Hart, he was looking for a person wielding the **MOST influence.**[1]

However, Masserman does not want us to depend on our fancies or prejudices: he wants to establish objective standards for judging, before we confer greatness upon anybody.

He says that **"Leaders must fulfil three functions - -"**

No. 1 THE LEADER MUST PROVIDE FOR THE WELL-BEING OF THE LEAD ...

---

1. Since Hart published his **"TOP 100"** many people have published books with the same theme. **"100 GREAT GOLFERS,"** or **"100 GREAT BATSMEN."** Many more will no doubt follow.

The leader, whoever he is, must be interested in your welfare. He must not be looking for milking cows for his own greed like the Rev. Jim Jones of Jonestown, Guyana, of the **"Suicide Cult"** fame. You will remember him as the man who committed suicide together with 910 of his followers, all at the same time **EN MASSE!**

The United States Government was on his trail and he was on the verge of being caught for certain felonies. But before they could apprehend him, he thought it wise to eliminate himself, together with all his followers, so that no one would be left to testify against him. He laced lemonade with cynide and inspired his devotees to drink it, and so they did and they all died in disgrace! In the meantime, it was discovered that the Rev. Jim Jones had salted away fifteen million dollars and stacked it in his own account in banks throughout the world. All his victims were his milking cows and he was exploiting them to satisfy his own lust and greed. Masserman's hero must be found to benefit his sheep, his flock, and not himself.

No. 2 THE LEADER OR WOULD BE LEADER MUST PROVIDE A SOCIAL ORGANIZATION IN WHICH PEOPLE FEEL RELATIVELY SECURE ...

Unlike the Marxist, the Facist, the Nazi, the Neo-Nazi, the Ashkenazi,[1] the Zionist, and their fellow-travellers, Professor Masserman, in his brief essay in the TIME magazine, did not spell this out. But his beliefs and feelings are abundantly clear. He is in search of a Leader who will provide a social order free of self, and greed and racism: for all these "isms" carry within them the seeds of their own destruction.

---

1. **Askhenazi:** the Jews from Germany, Central Europe and Eastern Europe, mostly from Russia who are in unlawful occupation of Palestine. There is something prophetic in the name itself — the Jews are doing to the people of the occupied territories exactly what the Nazis did to them. What an irony!

There's still with us much sorrow and sin,
Injustice, oppression, wrong and hate.
Still does Arrogance deaden Conscience,
Rob struggling souls of e'en the crumbs
Of Pity, and make, of loathsome flesh
And crumbling dust, fair-seeming Idols
For worship. Still does Ignorance blow
A mighty Horn and try to shame
True Wisdom. Still do men drive Slaves, - -
Protesting smoothly the end of Slavery!
Still does Greed devour the substance
Of helpless ones within her power.
Nay, more, - - the fine Individual Voice
Is smothered in the raucous din
Of groups and Crowds that madly shout
What they call Slogans New, - -
Old Falsehoods long discredited . . .

Abdullah Yusuf Ali

No. 3 THAT THIS LEADER MUST PROVIDE HIS PEOPLE WITH ONE SET OF BELIEFS . . .

It is easy to talk of the Fellowship of Faith and the Brotherhood of Man, but in South Africa today, there are a thousand different sects and denominations among the Whites (people of European descent) and three thousand among the Blacks (of African descent).

The White Churches in my country are spawning "Black" Bishops, fast, but in the first three hundred years of European conquest, they did not produce a single Black Bishop. Even now, the Black, the White, the Coloured and the Indian cannot pray together in most of the Dutch Reformed Churches. The hatred between the Christian sects was aptly described by the Christian Emperor Julian, who said:

"NO WILD BEASTS ARE SO HOSTILE TO MAN AS CHRISTIAN SECTS IN GENERAL ARE TO ONE ANOTHER."

Sayed Amir Ali in his ***"Spirit of Islam,"*** page lii.

With the foregoing three standards, Masserman searches history and analyses Louis Pasteur, Salk, Gandhi, Confucius, Alexander the Great, Caesar, Hitler, Buddha, Jesus and the rest;[1] finally coming to the conclusion that —

PERHAPS THE GREATEST LEADER OF ALL TIMES WAS MUHAMMED, WHO COMBINED ALL THREE FUNCTIONS. (and) TO A LESSER DEGREE, MOSES DID THE SAME

We cannot help marvelling at Masserman, that as a Jew he condescends to scrutinize even Adolf Hitler, the arch-enemy of his people. He considers Hitler to be a great leader. His race, the mighty German nation of 90 million people, was ready to march to destiny or destruction at his behest. Alas, he lead them to ruin.

Hitler is not the question. The question is why would Masserman, as an American Jew, a paid servant of the Government proclaim to his countrymen of over two hundred million Jews and Christians that **not** Jesus, **not** Moses **but** Muhummed[2] was **"The greatest Leader of all times!"** ACCOUNT FOR THAT!

WHAT SAY THE SCEPTICS?

Michael H. Hart put Muhummed No. 1 on his list and his own Lord and Saviour Jesus Christ (pbuh) No. 3.

Why? **"He was bribed!"** (?)

---

1. For Masserman's full essay see Appendix "C" on page 63.
2. Blessings of God on all His Messengers.

William McNeill considers Muhummed as worthy of honour in his list of the first three names of his.

Why? **"He was bribed!"** (?)

James Gavin puts Muhummed (pbuh) before Christ (pbuh). Why? **"He was bribed!"** (?)

James Masserman adjudges Muhummed (pbuh) No. 1 and his own hero Moses (pbuh) a close second.

Why? **"He was bribed"** (?)

> "ARE WE TO SUPPOSE THAT ALL THE GLOWING ADULATION OF MUHUMMED (PBUH) WAS A MISERABLE PIECE OF INTELLECTUAL LEGERDEMAIN, HOCUS POCUS . . . I, FOR MY PART, CANNOT FORM ANY SUCH SUPPOSITION . . . ONE WOULD BE ENTIRELY AT A LOSS WHAT TO THINK OF MANKIND AT ALL IF QUACKERY SO GREW AND FLOURISHED IN THE WORLD."[1]

Yet the scoffers bemoan anyone who has anything good to say about Muhummed (pbuh) or Islam AS HAVING BEEN BRIBED by the Arabs! They are giving too much credit to my bretheren. I repeat: **"It is possible, but it is improbable!"**

During the Second World War, Norway produced only one "Quisling."[2] He was tried for treason and executed. It is unlikely that America and the Western world have just reached puberty to spawn a breed of Quislings nurtured by hot petro-dollars from the Middle East. Please do not demean your honest, courageous men, who without fear or favour are prepared to suffer obloquy for their convictions. We must all admire them!

---

1. With apologies to Thomas Carlyle and his ***"Hero and Hero-worship."***

2. **"Quisling"** has come to mean a person who is a traitor to his nation and his country.

We can now justifiably conclude that the God of Mercy, Who forever recognises the sincere efforts of His servants, is only fulfilling His Promise to Muhummed (pbuh) His Chosen Messenger —

***AND HAVE WE NOT RAISED HIGH THE ESTEEM** (IN WHICH) **THOU** (ART HELD)?*

وَرَفَعْنَا لَكَ ذِكْرَكَ ۝

Holy Qur'an 94:4

Alternative renderings:[1]

(a) *Have We not exalted thy fame?*

(b) *And have We not raised thy name for thee?*

(c) *Have We not given you high renown?*

Friends and foe alike, as if by some secret compulsion are made to pay unsolicited tributes to this mighty Messenger of God. But the Almighty commandeers even the devil into His service, as He had done in the time of Jesus (pbuh), (Matthew 4:1-11). Even the devil sometimes speaks Gospel truths.

Professor K.S. Ramakrishna Rao, a Hindu philosopher, in his book **"MUHUMMED — The Prophet of Islam,"**[2] quotes the arch-devil himself, yes, Adolf Hitler, to prove the unique greatness of Muhummed (pbuh).

The Professor, like Jules Masserman who had evaluated the Prophet of Islam on three grounds (see appendix "C"

---

1. These quotes are from different translations of the Holy Qur'an. There are no separate "Versions" of the Holy Qur'an. For **"What is a Version,"** obtain my book — **"Is the Bible God's Word?"**

2. Obtainable **FREE** from the IPCI.

on page 63) also saw in Hitler's **"Mein Kampf"** a three-faceted jewel, a rare commodity which he found in our hero under discussion. Quoting Hitler, he says:

> "A GREAT THEORIST IS SELDOM A GREAT LEADER. AN AGITATOR IS FAR MORE LIKELY TO POSSESS THESE QUALITIES. HE WILL ALWAYS BE A BETTER LEADER. FOR, LEADERSHIP MEANS THE ABILITY TO MOVE MASSES OF MEN. THE TALENT TO PRODUCE IDEAS HAS NOTHING IN COMMON WITH THE CAPACITY FOR LEADERSHIP." HITLER CONTINUES, "THE UNION OF THE **THEORIST, ORGANISER,** AND **LEADER** IN ONE MAN IS THE RAREST PHENOMENON ON THIS EARTH; THEREIN CONSISTS GREATNESS." PROFESSOR RAO CONCLUDES, IN HIS OWN WORDS, **"IN THE PERSON OF THE PROPHET OF ISLAM THE WORLD HAS SEEN THIS RAREST PHENOMENON ON EARTH, WALKING IN FLESH AND BLOOD."**

SHARE THE ANGER

Before anyone assails the Professor of undue bias and **"bribery,"** let me give them a few more names of admirers of Muhummed (pbuh).

1. "MUHUMMAD WAS THE SOUL OF KINDNESS, AND HIS INFLUENCE WAS FELT AND NEVER FORGOTTEN BY THOSE AROUND HIM."

   A Hindu scholar — *Diwan Chand Sharma* in his **"The Prophets of the East,"** Calcutta 1935, p.122.

2. "FOUR YEARS AFTER THE DEATH OF JUSTINIAN, A.D. 569, WAS BORN AT MAKKAH, IN ARABIA THE MAN WHO, OF ALL MEN EXERCISED THE

GREATEST INFLUENCE[1] UPON THE HUMAN RACE ... MOHAMMED ..."

John William Draper, M.D., LLD., in his **"A History of the Intellectual Development of Europe,"** London 1875.

3. "I DOUBT WHETHER ANY MAN WHOSE EXTERNAL CONDITIONS CHANGED SO MUCH EVER CHANGED HIMSELF LESS TO MEET THEM."

R.V.C. Bodley in **"The Messenger,"** London 1946, p.9.

4. "I HAVE STUDIED HIM — THE WONDERFUL MAN — AND IN MY OPINION FAR FROM BEING AN ANTI-CHRIST, HE MUST BE CALLED THE SAVIOUR OF HUMANITY."

George Bernard Shaw, in **"The Genuine Islam,"** Vol. 1, No. 81936.

5. "BY A FORTUNE ABSOLUTELY UNIQUE IN HISTORY, MOHAMMED IS A THREEFOLD FOUNDER OF A NATION, OF AN EMPIRE, AND OF A RELIGION."

R. Bosworth-Smith in **"Mohammed and Mohammedanism,"** 1946.

6. "MOHAMMED WAS THE MOST SUCCESSFUL OF ALL RELIGIOUS PERSONALITIES."

Encyclopedia Britannica, 11th Edition

---

1. I wonder whether Michael H. Hart, as a historian, had stumbled across Draper's remark to inspire him to write his **"THE 100,"** a ranking of the Most Influential Persons in History? See page 3. Have you written for your **FREE** copy of the chapter on Muhummed (pbuh) from the **"TOP 100,"** yet?

CHAPTER 2

FROM THE HISTORICAL PAST

It is not difficult to reproduce a further dozen or more eulogies by the admirers and critics of Muhummed (pbuh). Despite all their objectivity, jaundiced minds can always conjure up some aspersions. Let me take my readers deep down in past history.

It was Friday the 8th of May, 1840, that is about a hundred and fifty years ago, at a time when it was a sacrilege to say anything good about Muhummed (pbuh), and the Christian West was trained to hate the man Muhummed (pbuh) and his religion, the same way as dogs were at one stage trained in my country to hate all black people.[1] At that time in history, Thomas Carlyle, one of the greatest thinkers of the past century delivered a series of lectures under the theme — **"Heroes and Hero-worship."**

DEVELOPED SICKNESS

Carlyle exposed this blind prejudice of his people at the beginning of his talk. He made reference to one of the literary giants a Dutch scholar and statesman, by the name of Hugo Grotius,[2] who had written a bitter and abusive invective against the prophet of Islam. He had falsely charged that the Holy Prophet had trained pigeons to pick out peas from his ears, so that he could by this trick bluff his people that the Holy Ghost in the shape of a dove was revealing God's Revelation to him, which he then had them

---

1. By the way **"dogs are colour blind!"** Yet it can be done.
2. From page 57 of the book — "On Heroes Hero-worship and the Heroic in History" by *Thomas Carlyle*, London 1959.

recorded in his Bible the Qur'an. Perhaps Grotius was inspired into this fairy-tale from his reading of his own Holy Scriptures:

> *Then Jesus, when he had been baptized* (by John the Baptist in the Jordan River), *came up immediately from the water; and behold, the heavens were opened to him, and he saw the* ***Spirit of God Descending Like A Dove*** *and alighting upon him.*
>
> (Emphasis added) Matthew 3:16

WHERE'S THE AUTHORITY

Pococke, another respected intellectual of the time, like "doubting Thomas" (John 20:25), wanted proof about Muhummed (pbuh), the pigeons, and the peas? Grotius answered "THAT THERE WAS NO PROOF!"

He just felt like inventing this story for his audience. To him and his audience the "pigeons and peas" theory was more plausible than that of the Archangel dictating to Muhummed (pbuh). These falsities wringed the heart of Carlyle. He cried:

> "THE LIES, WHICH WELL-MEANING ZEAL HAS HEAPED ROUND THIS MAN, ARE DISGRACEFUL TO OURSELVES ONLY."
>
> *Thomas Carlyle*

THE HERO PROPHET

Carlyle was a man of genius and God gifted him with the art of articulation. In his own way, he wanted to put the records straight. He planned to deliver a lecture and he chose a very provocative topic **"The Hero as Prophet."** and he chose this hero-prophet to be the most maligned man of his time, "MUHUMMED (PBUH)!" Not Moses, David, Solomon, or Jesus but Muhummed![1] To placate his overwhelming Anglican (belonging to the Church of England) fellow countrymen, he apologised —

> "AS THERE IS NO DANGER OF OUR BECOMING, ANY OF US, MAHOMETANS,[2] I MEAN TO SAY ALL THE GOOD OF HIM I JUSTLY CAN."

In other words he, as well as his elite audience, were free from the fear of converting to Islam, and could take a chance in paying some compliments to Muhummed (pbuh). If he had any fears regarding the strength of their faith, he would not have taken that chance.

In an era of hatred and spite towards everything Islamic and to an audience full of scepticism and cynicism, Carlyle unfolded many a glowing truth about his hero — Muhummed (pbuh). To the **"praise-worthy,"** indeed be praise. For that is what the very name Muhummed means — the Praised One — the Praiseworthy. There are times when Carlyle uses words and expressions which might not be too pleasing to the believing Muslim, but one has to forgive him as he was walking a cultural tightrope, and he succeeded eminently.

He paid our hero many ardent and enthusiastic tribute, and defended him from the false charges and calumnies of his enemies; exactly as the Prophet had done in the case of Jesus (pbuh) and his mother.[3]

---

1. May the Peace and Blessings of God be upon all his servants.
2. "Mahometans" means Muslims
3. See **"Muhummed the Natural Successor to Christ"** by the author.

HIS SINCERITY

1a. "THE GREAT MAN'S SINCERITY IS OF THE KIND HE CANNOT SPEAK OF: NAY, I SUPPOSE, HE IS CONSCIOUS RATHER OF **IN**-SINCERITY; FOR WHAT MAN CAN WALK ACCURATELY BY THE LAW OF TRUTH FOR ONE DAY? NO, THE GREAT MAN DOES NOT BOAST HIMSELF SINCERE, FAR FROM THAT; PERHAPS DOES NOT ASK HIMSELF IF HE IS SO: I WOULD SAY RATHER, HIS SINCERITY DOES NOT DEPEND ON HIMSELF: HE CANNOT HELP BEING SINCERE!"

Heros and Hero-Worship, p.59

b. "A SILENT GREAT SOUL; HE WAS ONE OF THOSE WHO CANNOT **BUT** BE IN EARNEST; WHOM NATURE HERSELF HAS APPOINTED TO BE SINCERE. WHILE OTHERS WALK IN FORMULAS AND HEARSAYS, CONTENTED ENOUGH TO DWELL THERE, THIS MAN COULD NOT SCREEN HIMSELF IN FORMULAS; HE WAS ALONE WITH HIS OWN SOUL AND THE REALITY OF THINGS . . . SUCH **SINCERITY**, AS WE NAMED IT, HAS IN VERY TRUTH SOMETHING OF DIVINE. THE WORD OF SUCH A MAN IS A VOICE DIRECT FROM NATURE'S OWN HEART. MEN DO AND MUST LISTEN TO THAT AS TO NOTHING ELSE; - - - ALL ELSE IS WIND IN COMPARISON."

Heros and Hero-Worship, p.71

In his lengthy speech Carlyle did not have the opportunity to inform his audience about the sources of his inferences. I may furnish just one incident from the life of the Prophet. An incidence which reflects the highest degree of his sincerity in recording a Revelation in the Holy Qur'an even if it seems to reprove him for some natural and human zeal.

ADMONITION AS REVEALED

It was in the early days of his mission in Makkah. Muhummed (pbuh) was deeply engrossed in trying to wean the leaders of the Pagan Quraish to his teachings. Apparently one of them was giving him an attentive hearing when a poor blind man by the name of **Abdullah ibn Umm-i-Maktum** tried to barge in into the discussion and wanting to draw attention to himself. The blessed Prophet said nothing, but a thought went through his mind (why don't you have a little patience, can't you see (sense) that because of your impatience I might lose these customers). I believe that lesser men, sinners and saints, will not be questioned for such lapses, but not so for Muhummed (pbuh). Did not God choose him and honour him with that lofty status as recorded?

And Most Certainly,
Thou (O MUHUMMED)
Art of most sublime
And Exalted Character.

Holy Qur'an 68:4

HE FROWNED

Whilst in the midst of the conversation with his pagan fellow tribesmen, God Almighty sends Gabriel, the Angel of Revelation, with this admonition:

(THE PROPHET) FROWNED AND TURNED AWAY, عَبَسَ وَتَوَلَّىٰٓ ۝

BECAUSE THERE CAME TO HIM THE BLIND MAN (INTERRUPTING). أَن جَآءَهُ ٱلْأَعْمَىٰ ۝

BUT WHAT COULD TELL THEE THAT PERCHANCE HE MIGHT GROW (IN SPIRITUAL UNDERSTANDING)?

وَمَا يُدْرِيكَ لَعَلَّهُ يَزَّكَّىٰٓ

OR THAT HE MIGHT RECEIVE ADMONITION, AND THE TEACHING MIGHT PROFIT HIM?

أَوْ يَذَّكَّرُ
فَتَنفَعَهُ ٱلذِّكْرَىٰٓ ۝

Holy Qur'an 80:1-4

The holy Prophet (pbuh) had naturally disliked the interruption. Perhaps the poor man's feelings were hurt. But he whose gentle heart ever sympathised with the poor and the afflicted, got new Light (Revelation) from his Lord, and without the least hesitation, he immediately published it for all eternity!

Subsequently, everytime he met this blind man, he received him graciously and thanked him that on his account the Lord had remembered him. During Muhummed's (pbuh) absences from Madinah, the blind man was made the Governor of the City twice. Such was the sincerity and gratitude of Carlyle's Hero Prophet.

HIS FIDELITY [1]

2. "IT IS A BOUNDLESS FAVOUR. — — — HE NEVER FORGOT THIS GOOD KADIJAH. LONG AFTERWARDS, AYESHA HIS YOUNG FAVOURITE WIFE, A WOMAN WHO INDEED DISTINGUISHED HERSELF AMONG THE MOSLEMS, BY ALL MANNER OF QUALITIES, THROUGH HER WHOLE LONG LIFE; THIS YOUNG BRILLIANT AYESHA WAS, ONE DAY, QUESTIONING HIM: 'NOW AM NOT I BETTER THAN KADIJAH? SHE WAS A

1. A few poetic verses on fidelity will be found in Appendix "D" page 63.

WIDOW; OLD, AND HAD LOST HER LOOKS: YOU LOVE ME BETTER THAN YOU DID HER?' — — — 'NO, BY ALLAH!' ANSWERED MAHOMET: 'NO, BY ALLAH! SHE BELIEVED IN ME WHEN NONE ELSE WOULD BELIEVE. IN THE WHOLE WORLD I HAD BUT ONE FRIEND, AND SHE WAS THAT!'"

Heroes and Hero-Worship, p. 76

It would have been easier to repel the temptation of the devil than to succumb to the ego of a young, loving, brilliant and beautiful wife like lady Ayesha Siddiqa. Why not let her hear the soft soothing balm of flattery; it will not harm anyone. Even the soul of Bibi Khadija, the mother of the Faithful, would look light-heartedly at the ruse. There is no shamming, no innocent "white lies" with Muhummed (pbuh). Traits of this kind show us the genuine man, brother of us all, brought visible through fourteen centuries, — — — the veritable son of our common mother.

<u>'AL AMEEN, THE FAITHFUL'</u>

3a. "A MAN OF TRUTH AND FIDELITY; TRUE IN WHAT HE DID, IN WHAT HE SPAKE AND THOUGHT. THEY NOTED THAT **HE** ALWAYS MEANT SOMETHING. A MAN RATHER TACITURN IN SPEECH; SILENT WHEN THERE WAS NOTHING TO BE SAID; BUT PERTINENT, WISE, SINCERE, WHEN HE DID SPEAK; ALWAYS THROWING LIGHT ON THE MATTER. THIS IS THE ONLY SORT OF SPEECH **WORTH** SPEAKING!"

Heros and Hero-Worship, p. 69

b. "MAHOMET NATURALLY GAVE OFFENCE TO THE **KOREISH**, **KEEPERS** OF THE **KAABAH**, SUPERINTENDENTS OF THE IDOLS. ONE OR TWO MEN OF INFLUENCE HAD JOINED HIM:

THE THING SPREAD SLOWLY, BUT IT WAS SPREADING, NATURALLY HE GAVE OFFENCE TO EVERYBODY."[1]

Heroes and Hero-Worship, p. 77

c. "NOT A MEALYMOUTHED MAN! A CANDID FEROCITY, IF THE CASE CALL FOR IT, IS IN HIM; HE DOES NOT MINCE MATTERS! THE WAR OF TABUC IS A THING HE OFTEN SPEAKS OF: HIS MEN REFUSED, MANY OF THEM, TO MARCH ON THAT OCCASION; PLEADED THE HEAT OF THE WEATHER, THE HARVEST, AND SO FORTH; HE CAN NEVER FORGET THAT. YOUR HARVEST? IT LASTS FOR A DAY. WHAT WILL BECOME OF YOUR HARVEST THROUGH ALL ETERNITY? HOT WEATHER? YES, IT WAS HOT; 'BUT HELL WILL BE HOTTER!' SOMETIMES A ROUGH SARCASM TURNS UP: HE SAYS TO THE UNBELIEVERS, YE SHALL NOT HAVE SHORT WEIGHT!"

Heros and Hero-Worship, p. 95/6.

Remember, Thomas Carlyle uttered these words, and many more to a shocked and bewildered Christian audience in England, a hundred and fifty years ago. History did not record for us the lively arguments and debates which his lecture must naturally have caused. He kept to his promise: **"I mean to say all the good of him** (his Hero Prophet) **I justly can,"** and he went on in his talk to defend Muhummed (pbuh) against the false charges, slander and calumnies of his enemies:

---

1. The Jews hated the Prophet: the Christians hated the Prophet: the ***Mushriks*** (the Polytheists) hated the Prophet, and the ***Munafiqeen*** (the hypocrites) hated the Prophet. It is the nature of Falsehood to hate the Truth. Light dismisses Darkness, but darkness does not take kindly to Light.

CHARGE OF FALSITY

4a. "A FALSE MAN FOUND A RELIGION? WHY, A FALSE MAN CANNOT BUILD A BRICK HOUSE! IF HE DOES NOT KNOW AND FOLLOW **TRULY** THE PROPERTIES OF MORTAR, BURNT CLAY AND WHAT ELSE HE WORKS IN, IT IS NO HOUSE THAT HE MAKES, BUT A RUBBISH HEAP. IT WILL NOT STAND FOR TWELVE CENTURIES,[1] TO LODGE A HUNDRED-AND-EIGHTY MILLIONS;[2] IT WILL FALL STRAIGHT-AWAY . . . SPECIOSITIES ARE SPECIOUS[3] . . . IT IS LIKE A FORGED BANK NOTE; THEY GET IT PASSED OUT OF **THEIR** WORTHLESS HANDS: OTHERS, NOT THEY, HAVE TO SMART FOR IT. NATURE BURSTS-UP IN FIRE-FLAMES, FRENCH REVOLUTIONS AND SUCH-LIKE, PROCLAIMING WITH THE TERRIBLE VERACITY THAT FORGED NOTES ARE FORGED."

Heros and Hero-Worship, p. 58

b. "IT GOES GREATLY AGAINST THE IMPOSTER THEORY, THE FACT THAT HE LIVED IN THIS ENTIRELY UNEXCEPTIONABLE, ENTIRELY QUIET AND COMMON PLACE WAY, TILL THE HEAT OF HIS YEARS WAS DONE. HE WAS FORTY BEFORE HE TALKED OF ANY MISSION FROM HEAVEN . . ALL HIS 'AMBITION,' SEEMINGLY, HAD BEEN, HITHERTO, TO LIVE AN HONEST LIFE; HIS 'FAME,' THE MERE GOOD OPINION OF NEIGHBOURS THAT KNEW HIM . . ."

Heros and Hero-Worship, p. 70

---

1. Now, fourteen centuries.
2. A thousand million today.
3. **Specious:** Having the ring of truth or plausibility but actually false.

c. "AMBITION? WHAT COULD ALL ARABIA DO FOR THIS MAN; WITH THE CROWN OF GREEK HERACLIUS, OF PERSIAN CHOSROES, AND ALL THE CROWNS IN EARTH; — WHAT COULD THEY ALL DO FOR HIM? IT WAS NOT OF THE HEAVEN ABOVE AND OF THE HELL BENEATH. ALL CROWNS AND SOVEREIGNTIES WHAT-SOEVER, WHERE WOULD **THEY** IN A FEW BRIEF YEARS BE? TO BE SHEIK OF MAKKAH OR ARABIA, AND HAVE A BIT OF GILT WOOD PUT INTO YOUR HAND, — — — WILL THAT BE ONES SALVATION? I DECIDEDLY THINK, NOT, WE WILL LEAVE IT ALTOGETHER, THIS IMPOSTER HYPOTHESIS, AS NOT CREDIT-ABLE; NOT VERY TOLERABLE EVEN, WORTHY CHIEFLY OF DISMISSAL BY US."

Heros and Hero-Worship, p. 72/3

CHARGE OF SINNING

5. "FAULTS? THE GREATEST OF FAULTS, I SHOULD SAY, IS TO BE CONSCIOUS OF NONE. READERS OF THE BIBLE ABOVE ALL, ONE WOULD THINK, MIGHT KNOW BETTER. WHO IS CALLED THERE 'THE MAN ACCORD-ING TO GOD'S OWN HEART'? DAVID, THE HEBREW KING HAD FALLEN INTO SINS ENOUGH; BLACKEST CRIMES; THERE WAS NO WANT OF SINS.[1] AND THEREUPON THE UNBELIEVERS SNEER AND ASK, IS THIS YOUR MAN ACCORDING TO GOD'S HEART? THE SNEER, I MUST SAY, SEEMS TO ME BUT A

1. This is the Jewish and Christian concept of God's prophets. They charge their prophets with incest, adultery and even murder. They impute horrendous crimes to them on the authority of the Holy Bible.

SHALLOW ONE. WHAT ARE FAULTS, WHAT ARE THE OUTWARD DETAILS OF A LIFE; IF THE INNER SECRET OF IT, THE REMORSE, TEMPTATIONS, TRUE, OFTEN-BAFFLED, NEVER-ENDED STRUGGLE OF IT BE FORGOTTEN? 'IT IS NOT IN MAN THAT WALKETH TO DIRECT HIS STEPS.' OF ALL ACTS, IS NOT, FOR A MAN, **REPENTANCE** THE MOST DIVINE? THE DEADLIEST SIN, I SAY, WERE THE SAME SUPER-CILIOUS CONSCIOUSNESS OF NO SIN; THAT IS DEATH; THE HEART SO CONSCIOUS IS DIVORCED FROM SINCERITY, HUMILITY, AND FACT; IS DEAD: IT IS 'PURE' AS DEAD DRY SAND IS PURE."

Heros and Hero-Worship, p. 61

CHARGE OF "THE SWORD"

The greatest crime, the greatest "sin" of Muhummed (pbuh) in the eyes of the Christian West is that he did not allow himself to be slaughtered, to be "crucified" by his enemies. He ably defended himself, his family and his followers; and finally vanquished his enemies. Muhummed's (pbuh) success is the Christians' gall of disappointment: he did not believe in any vicarious sacrifice for the sins of others. He believed and behaved naturally. **IN THE STATE OF NATURE, EVERYONE HAS A RIGHT TO DEFEND HIS PERSON AND POSSESSIONS, AND EXTEND HIS HOSTILITIES TO A REASONABLE AMOUNT OF SATISFACTION AND RETALIATION,"** says Gibbon, the master historian in his ***"Decline and Fall of the Roman Empire."*** His struggle and victory over the forces of unbelief and evil made the editors of the Encyclopedia Britannica to exclaim, Muhummed (pbuh) to be — — — **"THE MOST SUCCESSFUL OF ALL RELIGIOUS PERSONALITIES."**

How can the enemies of Islam account for Muhummed's phenomenal achievements except to decry that he spread his religion at the point of the sword? He forced Islam down peoples' throats!?

6a. "HISTORY MAKES IT CLEAR HOWEVER, THAT THE LEGEND OF FANATICAL MUSLIMS SWEEPING THROUGH THE WORLD AND FORCING ISLAM AT THE POINT OF THE SWORD UPON CONQUERED RACES IS ONE OF THE MOST FANTASTICALLY ABSURD MYTHS THAT HISTORIANS HAVE EVER REPEATED."

De Lacy O'Leary in
"Islam at the Crossroads" London, 1923, p.8

You do not have to be a historian like O'Leary to know that the Muslims ruled Spain for 736 years. The longest the Christians ever ruled over Muslims was 500 years in Mozambique, a territory captured from an Arab governor by the name of **Musa-bin-baique**, a name they could not properly pronounce, hence the name Mozambique. Even today, after five centuries of Christian overlordship the country is still 60 percent Muslim.

However, after eight centuries in Spain the Muslims were totally eliminated from that country so that not even one man was left to give the **Azaan** (the Muslim call to prayer). If the Muslim had used force, military or economic there would not have been any Christian left in Spain to have kicked the Muslims out. One can blame the Muslim for exploitation if you like but one cannot charge them with using the sword to convert Spaniards to the Islamic religion.

Today, Islam is still spreading all over the world — and Muslims have NO sword!![1]

---

1. See chart on page 34, **"the fastest growing faith on earth"**.

The Muslims were also the masters of India for a thousand years, but eventually when the sub-continent received independence in 1947, the Hindus obtained three-quarters of the country and the Muslims the balance of the one-quarter. Why? Because the Muslims did not force Islam down the Hindus' throat! In Spain and in India, the Muslims were no paragons of virtue, yet they obeyed the Qur'anic injunction to the letter —

LET THERE BE NO COMPULSION IN RELIGION: لَآ إِكْرَاهَ فِي الدِّينِ

FOR TRUTH STANDS OUT DISTINCT FROM ERROR: قَد تَّبَيَّنَ الرُّشْدُ مِنَ الْغَيِّ

Holy Qur'an 2:256

The Muslim conquerors understood from this command that "compulsion" was incompatible with true religion: because

(a) Religion depends on faith and will, and these would be meaningless if induced by force. Force can conquer but cannot convert.

(b) Truth and Error have been so clearly shown up by the Mercy of God that there should be no doubt in the minds of any person of goodwill as to the fundamentals of faith.

(c) God's protection is continuous and His Plan is always to lead us from the depths of darkness into the clearest light.[1]

Except for some eccentrics here and there, the Muslims as a whole adhered to the commandment of God in the lands over which they held sway.

---

1. (a), (b) and (c) are Yusuf Ali's comments on verse 256. Obtain his translation with over 6000 explanatory footnotes from the IPCI.

But what can the enemy say about countries where no single Muslim soldier had set foot?

(i) INDONESIA: It is a fact that over a hundred million Indonesians are Muslim, yet no conquering Muslim army ever landed on any of its over two thousand islands.

(ii) MALAYSIA: The overwhelming number of its people in this country are Muslims yet no Muslim soldier had landed there either.

(iii) AFRICA: The majority of the people on the East coast of Africa as far down as Mozambique, as well as the bulk of the inhabitants on the West coast of the continent are Muslims, but history does not record any invading hoards of Muslims from anywhere. What sword? Where was the sword? The Muslim trader did the job. His good conduct and moral rectitude achieved the miracle of conversion.

"All what you say seems incontrovertible, Mr. Deedat," says the Christian controversialist, "but we are talking about Islam at its very beginning, the way in which your prophet converted the pagans to his faith! How did he do it if not with the sword?"

ONE AGAINST ALL?

We can do no better than to allow Thomas Carlyle himself to defend his Hero Prophet against this false charge; — — —

7. "THE SWORD INDEED: BUT WHERE WILL YOU GET YOUR SWORD! EVERY NEW OPINION, AT

ITS STARTING, IS PRECISELY IN A **MINORITY OF ONE.** IN ONE MAN'S HEAD ALONE, THERE IT DWELLS AS YET. ONE MAN ALONE OF THE WHOLE WORLD BELIEVES IT; THERE IS ONE MAN AGAINST ALL MEN. THAT HE TAKE A SWORD, AND TRY TO PROPAGATE WITH THAT, WILL DO LITTLE FOR HIM. YOU MUST FIRST GET YOUR SWORD! ON THE WHOLE, A THING WILL PROPAGATE ITSELF AS IT CAN. WE DO NOT FIND, OF THE CHRISTIAN RELIGION EITHER, THAT IT ALWAYS DISDAINED THE SWORD, WHEN ONCE IT HAD GOT ONE. CHARLEMAGNE'S CONVERSION OF THE SAXONS WAS NOT BY PREACHING."

Heros and Hero-Worship, p. 80

At the age of forty when Muhummed (pbuh) declared his mission from heaven, there was no political party, or royalty, and certainly no family or tribe to back him up. His people — the Arabs, immersed in idol-worship and fetishism were not by any means a docile people, they were no easy meat. They were a very volatile people. given to internecine and fratricidal wars: subject to **"all kinds of fierce sincerities"** (Carlyle). One man, single-handed, to wean such a people required nothing short of a miracle. A miracle did happen. God alone could have made Islam and Muhummed (pbuh) to triumph through with flimsy, gossamer support. God fulfilling His promise:

And have We not raised high the esteem (in which) thou (O Muhummed art held)?

Holy Qur'an 94:4

CHAPTER 3

FASTEST GROWING RELIGION TODAY

THE SWORD OF THE INTELLECT

The enemy, the sceptic, the missionary and their passive camp followers will not stop bleating that "Islam was spread at the point of the sword!" but they will not venture to answer our question — — "WHO BRIBED CARLYLE!?" In 1840 when Carlyle defended Muhummed (pbuh) and refuted the allegation about the sword, there was nobody around to bribe. The whole Muslim world was in the gutters. The countries of Islam were all under subjugation by the Christians, except for a few like — Persia, Afghanistan and Turkey who were only nominally independent. There were no riches to flaunt and no petro-dollars to bribe with!

That was yesterday and many yesterdays ago, but what about today, in modern times? It is claimed **from the chart on the next page** that "Islam is the fastest growing religion in the world." The overall increase of all the sects and denominations of Christianity was a staggering 138 per cent with the incredible increase of Islam by 235 per cent in the same period of time of half-a-century. It is further affirmed that in Britain and the United States of America, islam is the fastest growing faith. It is said that in Britain **"There are more Muslims than Methodists in the coun-try."** You have a right to ask, "What sword?" The answer is, "THE SWORD INDEED!" (Thomas Carlyle)[1] **It is the sword of intellect!** It is the fulfilment of yet another prophecy;—

---

1. See full quote on page 31, No 7

A CRUCIAL HALF CENTURY OF RELIGION

by Keith W. Stump

We highlight the most significant developments.

WORLD'S MAJOR RELIGIONS 1934/1984

NUMBER OF ADHERENTS IN 1934*   NUMBER OF ADHERENTS IN 1984#

Religion	1934	1984	Change
BUDDHISM	150,180,000	245,000,000	63% INCREASE
CHRISTIANITY	682,400,000	1,000,000,000	47% INCREASE
ROMAN CATHOLIC	331,500,000	565,000,000	70% INCREASE
PROTESTANT	206,900,000	324,000,000	57% INCREASE
EASTERN ORTHODOX	144,000,000	92,000,000	36% DECREASE
CONFUCIANISM & TAOISM	350,600,000	305,000,000	13% DECREASE
HINDUISM	230,150,000	500,000,000	117% INCREASE
ISLAM	209,020,000	700,000,000	235% INCREASE
JUDAISM	15,630,000	15,000,000	4% DECREASE
SHINTOISM	25,000,000	63,000,000	152% INCREASE

*Source: The World Almanac and Book of Facts, 1935.
#Source: The Reader's Digest Almanac and Yearbook, 1983.

The PLAIN TRUTH

هُوَ الَّذِىٓ اَرۡسَلَ رَسُوۡلَهٗ بِالۡهُدٰى وَدِيۡنِ الۡحَـقِّ لِيُظۡهِرَهٗ عَلَى الدِّيۡنِ كُلِّهٖ ؕ وَكَفٰى بِاللّٰهِ شَهِيۡدًا ؕ

IT IS HE** (God Almighty) **WHO HAS SENT HIS MESSENGER** (Muhummed) **WITH GUIDANCE

***AND THE RELIGION OF TRUTH** (Islam)*

THAT HE MAY MAKE IT PREVAIL OVER ALL RELIGIONS,

AND ENOUGH IS GOD FOR A WITNESS.

Holy Qur'an 48:28

The destiny of Islam is spelt out here in the clearest terms. Islam is to master, overcome and supersede every other faith —

> *That He* (God Almighty) ***make it*** (Islam) *prevail over all religions . . .*

In Arabic the word is ***Deen*** [1] (literally meaning "Way of Life"), to supersede all, whether it be Hinduism, Buddhism, Christianism,[2] Judaism, Communism or any other **"Ism."** This is the destiny of Allah's ***Deen.***

The same Qur'anic Verse is repeated in chapter 61 verse 9 which ends with this slight variation —

> (Never mind) *Though the unbelievers might be averse to it* (Islam).

TRIUMPH OF ISLAM

Islam will prevail. It is the promise of God, and His Promise is true. But how? With the sword? Not even if we had the laser gun! Could we use it? The Holy Qur'an forbids us to use force as a means of converting! Yet the verse

---

1. Usually translated as Religion, which literally Islam is not.
2. In the time of Thomas Carlyle this was the term applied to Christianity.

prophesies that Islam would be the most dominant of all religions. The triumphs of its doctrines have already started and is gaining hold over the religious ideology and doctrines of the various schools of thought in the world. Though not in the name of Islam, but in the name of reformation and amendments, the doctrines of Islam are being fastly grafted into the various religious orders. Many things which are exclusively Islamic and which were formerly unknown, or which were being opposed before with tooth and nail by the other creeds, are now part of their believes.

The Brotherhood of man
The abolition of the Caste system and untouchability
The right of women to inherit
Opening the places of worship to all
Prohibition of all intoxicants
The true concept of the Unity of God etc, etc.

Just one word on the last subject above, before we proceed further. Ask any theist, polytheist,[1] pantheist,[2] or trinitarian: how many Gods he believes in? He will shudder to say anything other than ONE! This is the EFFECT of the strict monotheism of Islam.

> THE CREED OF MOHAMED IS FREE FROM THE SUSPICIONS OF AMBIGUITY AND THE KORAN IS A GLORIOUS TESTIMONY TO THE UNITY OF GOD.
>
> *Gibbon* in his
> **"Decline and Fall of the Roman Empire."**

VERDICT OF NON-MUSLIM ORIENTALS

Almost all the defenders of Muhummed (pbuh) who spoke out against the false theory that he spread his religion

---

1. **Polytheist:** One who believes in many gods.
2. **Pantheist:** The one who believes that everything is god. Of course the **"trinitarian,"** you already know.

at the point of the sword, were Westerners. Let us now hear what some non-Muslim Easterners have to say on the subject:

8a. THE MORE I STUDY THE MORE I DISCOVER THAT THE STRENGTH OF ISLAM DOES NOT LIE IN THE SWORD.

Mahatma Gandhi — the father of modern India, in **"Young India."**

b. THEY (Muhummed's critics) SEE FIRE INSTEAD OF LIGHT, UGLINESS INSTEAD OF GOOD. THEY DISTORT AND PRESENT EVERY GOOD QUALITY AS A GREAT VICE. IT REFLECTS THEIR OWN DEPRAVITY...
THE CRITICS ARE BLIND. THEY CANNOT SEE THAT THE ONLY 'SWORD' MUHAMMAD WIELDED WAS THE SWORD OF MERCY, COMPASSION, FRIENDSHIP AND FORGIVENESS — THE SWORD THAT CONQUERS ENEMIES AND PURIFIES THEIR HEARTS. HIS SWORD WAS SHARPER THAN THE SWORD OF STEEL.

Pandit Gyanandra Dev Sharma Shastri, at a meeting in Gorakhpur (India). 1928

c. HE PREFERRED MIGRATION TO FIGHTING HIS OWN PEOPLE, BUT WHEN OPPRESSION WENT BEYOND THE PALE OF TOLERANCE HE TOOK UP HIS SWORD IN SELF-DEFENCE. THOSE WHO BELIEVE RELIGION CAN BE SPREAD BY FORCE ARE FOOLS WHO NEITHER KNOW THE WAYS OF RELIGION NOR THE WAYS OF THE WORLD. THEY ARE PROUD OF THIS BELIEF BECAUSE THEY ARE A LONG, LONG WAY AWAY FROM THE TRUTH.

A Sikh journalist in **"Nawan Hindustan,"** Delhi, 17 November 1947.

It was Rudyard Kipling who said, **"East is East and West is West, never the twain shall meet!"** He was wrong! In the defence of Muhummed (pbuh), **all,** who are not blinded by prejudice will converge.

THREE OTHER STANDARDS

Fourteen years after Thomas Carlyle had delivered his lecture on his **Hero Prophet,** a Frenchman by the name of Lamartine wrote the history of the Turks. Incidentally, the Turks being Muslims, Lamartine touched on some aspects of Islam and its founder. Like our Jules Masserman (see page 10) of current times, who had conceived three objective standards for discovering greatness of leadership; Lamartine had over a century ago thought of **three** other objective standards for conferring **GREATNESS.** We must give credit to the Westerner for this type of insight. Lamartine opines:

9. **IF GREATNESS OF PURPOSE, SMALLNESS OF MEANS AND ASTOUNDING RESULTS**[1] ARE THE THREE CRITERIA OF HUMAN GENIUS, WHO COULD DARE TO COMPARE ANY GREAT MAN IN MODERN HISTORY WITH MUHUMMED? (Lamartine ends his lengthy segment of literary masterpiece with the words): . . . PHILOSOPHER, ORATOR, APOSTLE, LEGISLATOR, WARRIOR, CONQUEROR OF IDEAS, RESTORER OF RATIONAL BELIEFS, OF A CULT WITHOUT IMAGES: THE FOUNDER OF TWENTY TERRESTRIAL EMPIRES AND OF ONE SPIRITUAL EMPIRE, THAT IS MUHUMMED. **AS REGARDS ALL STANDARDS BY WHICH HUMAN GREATNESS MAY BE MEASURED, WE MAY WELL ASK, IS THERE ANY MAN GREATER THEN HE?**

Lamartine, **"Historie de la Turquie,"** Paris 1854

---

1. The full quotation from Larmartine's book will be found in appendix "B" page 61

The answer to his question, **"Is there any man greater than he?"** is reposed in the question itself. By implication he is saying . . . **"there is no man greater than Muhummed. Muhummed is the greatest man that ever lived!"**

And have We not raised high the esteem (in which) thou (O Muhummed art held)?

Holy Qur'an 94:4

MOST CERTAINLY THOU HAST, O, MY LORD!

Before we absolve Lamartine of any favouritism, partiality, or of the charge of being bribed, we will scrutinize his three standards, and whether they can be justified in the case of Muhummed (pbuh).

1. GREATNESS OF PURPOSE

History of the time will tell you that it was the darkest period in the history of mankind when Muhummed (pbuh) was commanded to declare his mission. The need was for the raising of prophets in every corner of the world, or the sending of one Master Messenger for the whole of mankind, to deliver them from falsehood, superstition, selfishness, polytheism, wrong and oppression. It was to be the reclamation of the whole of humanity. And God Almighty in His wisdom chose His prophet from the backwaters of Arabia as His universal Messenger. Thus He records in His Noble Book —

وَمَآ أَرْسَلْنَٰكَ إِلَّا
رَحْمَةً لِّلْعَٰلَمِينَ ۝

AND WE SENT THEE NOT *(O Muhummed),*
BUT AS A MERCY
UNTO *(all)* ***THE WORLDS.***

Holy Qur'an 21:107

"There is no question now of race or nation, of a "chosen people" or the "seed of Abraham,"; or the "seed of David"; or of Hindu Arya varta; of

Jew or Gentile. Arab or 'Ajam (Persian), Turk or Tajik, European or Asiatic, White or Coloured; Aryan, Semitic, Mongolian, or African; or American, Australian, or Polynesian. To all men and creatures who have any spiritual responsibilty, the principles universally apply."

Abdullah Yusuf Ali [1]

JESUS (PBUH) DISCRIMINATES

Muhummed's (pbuh) immediate predecessor advised his disciples, **"Give not that which is holy unto the dogs"** (meaning non-Jews), **"Neither cast ye your pearls before swine"** (meaning non-Jews, Matthew 7:6). The Gospel writers are unanimous in recording that Christ lived by the precepts which he preached. In his lifetime he did not preach to a single non-Jew. In fact he spurned a gentile woman who sought his spiritual blessings (**"the woman was a Greek"** Mark 7:26). Then during the "passover" season in Jerusalem when the master with his disciples had congregated for the occasion, certain Greeks hearing of his reputation sought an audience with him for spiritual enlightenment, but Jesus (pbuh) gave them the "cold shoulder" [2] as narrated by St. John:

And there were certain Greeks among them that came up to worship at the feast:

The same came therefore to Philip . . . and desired him saying, Sir, we would see Jesus.

---

1. Get your copy now of Yusuf Ali's, English translation and commentary, with over 6000 annotations. Obtain a copy for your non-Muslim friend, also.

2. Means: a deliberately unkind or unfriendly treatment; a slight; a snub.

Philip cometh and telleth Andrew: and again Andrew and Philip tell Jesus.

John 12:20-22

SELF GLORIFICATION

The verses that follow do not even record the courtesy of **"Yea,yea;"** or **"Nay, nay;"** (Yes, yes or no, no of Matthew 5:37). They continue with his own praise —

And Jesus answered them (Andrew and Philip), *saying, The hour is come, that the son of man* (referring to himself) *should be glorified.*

John 12:23

HIGHEST STANDARDS

Muhummed (pbuh) could never afford any such latitudes. Remember, how the Almighty reminded him of the highest etiquette required from him. Even the thought of being ruffled by the untimely intrusion of a blind man, was not accepted from him (see page 22 **"He frowned"**). As a universal Messenger, God set for him the most lofty standards:

And Most Certainly,
Thou (O MUHUMMED)
Art of most sublime
And Exalted Character.

Holy Qur'an 68:4

And his diocese, his field of mission? The whole of mankind!

And We sent thee not (O Muhummed), but as a Mercy unto (all) the worlds.

Holy Qur'an 21:107

UNIVERSAL MESSENGER

These are not mere platitudes; beautiful sentiments bereft of action. Muhummed (pbuh) practised what he preached. Among his first ***Sahábás*** (companions) and converts, beside the Arab can be counted **Bilal** the Abyssinian, **Salman** the Persian and **Abdullah Bin-Salaam** the Jew. The sceptics may say that his outreach was simply incidental but what can they say about the historical fact that before his demise, he sent out five epistles, one to each of the five surrounding countries, inviting them to accept the religion of Islam.

1. The Emperor of Persia
2. The King of Egypt
3. The Negus of Abyssinia
4. The Emperor Hiraclius at Constantinople, and
5. The King of Yemen

Thus he set the example for the fulfilment of his impelling mission, his **"greatness of purpose,"** the reclamation of the whole of humanity into the Master's fold. Is there another example of such universality in another religion? Muhummed (pbuh) was not out to set or to break any records, he was simply carrying out the trust that was reposed in him by the Lord of Creation!

2. SMALLNESS OF MEANS

Muhummed (pbuh) was born with no silver spoon in his mouth. His life begins with infinitesimal support. His father had died before he was born. His mother dies by the time he was six years old. He was doubly-orphaned at this tender age, his grandfather Abdul-Muttalib takes charge of the child, but within three years he also died. As soon as he was able, he began to look after his uncle Abu Talib's sheep and goats for his keep. Contrast this poor, double-orphaned Arab child with some of the great religious personalities that preceded him, and you must marvel at what Destiny had in store for him!

Abraham (pbuh) the spiritual father of Moses, Jesus and Muhummed (May the peace of God be upon them all), was the son of a very successful businessman of his time. Moses (pbuh) was reared in the house of Pharoah. Jesus (pbuh) though described as **"a carpenter and the son of a carpenter,"** was well endowed with learning as well as material means. Peter, Philip, Andrew, etc. all downed tools and followed him to be at his beck and call, not because he had any **halo**[1] on his head; there was no such thing, but because of his affluent attire and princely bearing. He could command mansions in Jerusalem for himself and his disciples even during the height of the festive season; and have sumptuous suppers arranged; and you could hear him reproach the materialistic Jews —

> *And when they found him (Jesus) on the other side of the sea, they said to him, "Rabbi, when did you come here?"*
>
> *Jesus answered them and said, "most assuredly, I say to you, you seek me,*

---

1. **Halo:** An imaginary luminous ring or disc surrounding the head of saintly men and women in religious paintings.

not because you saw the signs,[1] *but because you ate of the loaves and were filled.*

John 6:25-26

NOTHING TO OFFER

Muhummed (pbuh) had no bread nor meat to offer; no sugar-plums of any kind, in this world or the next! The only thing he could offer his bedraggled, poor shepherd people was trial and tribulations and the strait-jacketing of their lives here on earth and the good pleasures of God in the Hereafter. The life of the Prophet was an open book before them. He had shown them as to what he was; the nobility of his character, his integrity of purpose, his earnestness and fiery enthusiasm for the truth he had come to preach revealed the hero; and they followed him. Mr. Stanley Lane Poole's estimate of our hero is so beautiful and yet so truthful that I cannot resist the temptation of quoting it here:

> HE WAS AN ENTHUSIAST IN THAT NOBLEST SENSE WHEN ENTHUSIASM BECOMES THE SALT OF THE EARTH, THE ONE THING THAT KEEPS MEN FROM ROTTING WHILST THEY LIVE.
>
> ENTHUSIASM IS OFTEN USED DESPITEFULLY, BECAUSE IT IS JOINED TO AN UNWORTHY CAUSE, OR FALLS UPON BARREN GROUND AND BEARS NO FRUIT. SO WAS IT NOT WITH MOHAMMED. HE WAS AN ENTHUSIAST WHEN ENTHUSIASM WAS THE ONE THING NEEDED TO SET THE WORLD AFLAME, AND HIS ENTHUSIASM WAS NOBLE FOR A NOBLE CAUSE.

---

1. The veracity of the Messiah's message and his mission.

HE WAS ONE OF THOSE HAPPY FEW WHO HAVE ATTAINED THE SUPREME JOY OF MAKING ONE GREAT TRUTH THEIR VERY LIFE-SPRING.

HE WAS THE MESSENGER OF THE ONE GOD; AND NEVER TO HIS LIFE'S END DID HE FORGET WHO HE WAS, OR THE MESSAGE WHICH WAS THE MARROW OF HIS BEING. HE BROUGHT HIS TIDINGS TO HIS PEOPLE WITH A GRAND DIGNITY SPRUNG FROM THE CONSCIOUSNESS OF HIS HIGH OFFICE, TOGETHER WITH A MOST SWEET HUMILITY, WHOSE ROOTS LAY IN THE KNOWLEDGE OF HIS OWN WEAKNESS."

It may easliy be conceded that Muhummed (pbuh) was blessed with the flimsiest of human resources. In fact the odds were loaded against him. But what about his fortune towards the end of his earthly sojourn? He was the overlord of the whole of Arabia! What about the endless means at his disposal then? We will allow a Christian missionary to answer that —

HE WAS CAESAR AND POPE IN ONE; BUT HE WAS POPE WITHOUT THE POPE'S PRETENTIONS, AND CAESAR WITHOUT THE LEGIONS OF CAESAR: WITHOUT A STANDING ARMY, WITHOUT A BODYGUARD, WITHOUT A PALACE, WITHOUT A FIXED REVENUE; IF EVER ANY MAN HAD THE RIGHT TO SAY THAT HE RULED BY THE RIGHT DIVINE, IT WAS MOHAMMAD, FOR HE HAD ALL THE POWERS WITHOUT ITS INSTRUMENTS AND WITHOUT ITS SUPPORTS."

R. Bosworth Smith
"Mohammad and Mohammadanism", London 1874, p. 92

HIS HANDICAPS

His "weakness" was his strength. The very fact that he had no material means of support made him to put his entire trust in God, and God the Merciful did not forsake him. His success was all the more staggering. May not the Muslims justly say, the entire work was the work of God? **And Muhummed (pbuh) his instrument?**

3. OUTSTANDING RESULTS

In the words of Thomas Carlyle — **"One man against all men,"**[1] to a hundred and twenty four thousand at the Farewell Pilgrimage alone. How many were left behind of men, women and children, believers all?

On the 12th of RABI I., in the 11th year after the ***Hijra,***[2] approximating to the 8th of June 632 of the Christian Era, whilst praying earnestly in whisper, the spirit of the great Prophet took flight to the **"blessed companionship on high"** *(Ibn Hisham).*

Hazrat Omar (May Allah be pleased with him), on receiving the sad news of the demise of the Holy Prophet, lost his bearings. He was so shocked that he blurted out "If anyone says that Muhummed is dead, I will chop off his head!" Hazrat Abu Bakr As-Siddiq presently verified that the Master had indeed departed from this world; and coming out from the Prophet's apartment announced to the gathering throng outside, that, **"Muhummed (pbuh) had indeed passed away. Those that worshipped Muhummed,"** he said, **"Let them know that Muhummed is dead, but those who worship Allah, let them know that Allah lives for ever!"**

---

1. See full quotation by Thomas Carlyle on page 31.
2. ***Hijra:*** literally means Migration.

This brought Omar al-Farooq (R.A.) back to his senses. Could this man who was to become the second great ***Khaleefah*** of Islam at this moment imagine that fourteen hundred years later there would be a **thousand million** followers of Muhummed (pbuh) at one time? Could he have visualized that the religion of the Prophet would be the fastest growing religion in the world?[1]

Christianity had a 600-year start on Islam. Numerically the Christians claim to outnumber the followers of any other faith; this is true but let us look at the picture in its true perspective —

> THERE ARE MORE **PROFESSING** CHRISTIANS IN THE WORLD THAN **PROFESSING** MUSLIMS, BUT THERE ARE MORE **PRACTISING** MUSLIMS IN THE WORLD THAN **PRACTISING** CHRISTIANS.
> (Emphasis added)

R.V.C. Bodley (the American) in
"The Messenger: The Life of Mohammed." U.S.A. 1969

I understand from the above that Mr. Bodley is trying to tell us that there are people in the world who, when filling their census forms, will tick off the term **Christian** under "Religion." It is not necessarily that they believe in the dogmas of Christianity. They could actually be atheists or **bush-Baptists,**[2] as opposed to being a Jew or Hindu or Muslim; coming from a Christian background they would for the purpose of convenience label themselves **"Christian."** From that point of view, and from the point of view that a person who practises what he believes, there would be more Muslims in the world than Christians.

---

1. See chart on page 34
2. **"bush-Baptist":** There are forty different Baptist Churches in the United States of America. But bush-Baptists are people with strong religious feelings yet will not go to any Church; and will not affiliate with any sect or denomination.

Chronologically, Islam is six hundred years behind Christianity, but amazingly it is at least a very close second, and is catching up fast — the fastest growing religion in the world today (see chart on page 34). **"One Billion!"** The figure is outstanding and the sincerity and practise of the Believers astonishing!

Taking into account his own three objective standards: (a) **"greatness of purpose;"** (b) **"smallness of means;"** and (c) **"outstanding results;"** does Lamartine dare to produce another candidate greater than Muhummed (pbuh)? He further awes his readers with the multifarious roles of Muhummed (pbuh) in which he excelled, ie. **Philosopher, Orator, Apostle, Legislator, Warrior, Conqueror of Ideas, the Restorer of Rational Beliefs, of a Cult without Images, the Founder of twenty Terrestrial Empires and of one Spiritual Empire, that is Muhummed. As regards ALL standards** (I repeat "ALL") **by which Human Greatness may be measured, we may well ask, "IS THERE ANY MAN GREATER THAN HE?"** (Emphasis added).

No! Muhummed (pbuh) was the greatest man that ever lived! According to Lamartine the French historian. And God Almighty questions —

And have We not raised high
the esteem (in which) thou
(O Muhummed art held)?

Holy Qur'an 94:4

MOST ASSUREDLY THOU HAST, O MY LORD!

THE QUALITY OF MERCY

The Christian propagandists make the wild boast that there is nothing in the history of mankind to compare with the merciful and forgiving cry of Jesus (pbuh) on the cross . . .

"Father, forgive them, for they know not what they do."

Luke 23:34

Amazing as it may sound, of the four writers of the Canonical Gospels, only St. Luke was inspired by the Holy ghost (?) to pen these words. The other three — Matthew, Mark and John never heard these words or they felt them to be too insipid or not important enough for recording. St. Luke was not even one of the twelve disciples selected by Jesus (pbuh). According to the revisers of the Revised Standard Version (RSV) of the Bible, these words are not in the most ancient manuscripts which by implication means that they are an interpolation.

In **"The New King James Version,"** (Copyrighted by the Thomas Nelson Publishers in 1984), we are told that these words are **"not in the original text"** of the Greek manuscripts of St. Luke. In other words they have been fabricated by some pious gentleman. Although the quotation is unauthentic, we will still entertain it because it demonstrates great piety of loving one's enemies and of unsurpassed forgiveness as preached by the Master himself.

For forgiveness to be of any worth, the forgiver must be in a position to forgive. If the victim of injustice is still in the clutches of his enemies; in that helpless position and he would cry out, "I FORGIVE YOU!" it would be meaningless. But if the aggrieved party had turned the tables on his enemies and was in a position of taking revenge or exact retribution, and yet say "I forgive you!", only then would it mean something!

MUHUMMED'S (PBUH) CLEMENCY

Contrast the alleged forgiveness from the "cross" with the historical bloodless conquest of Makkah by Muhummed (pbuh) at the head of ten thousand "saints"[1] (his companions).

> "THE CITY WHICH HAD TREATED HIM SO CRUELLY, DRIVEN HIM AND HIS FAITHFUL BAND FOR REFUGE AMONGST STRANGERS, WHICH HAD SWORN HIS LIFE AND THE LIVES OF HIS DEVOTED DISCIPLES, LAY AT HIS FEET. HIS OLD PERSECUTERS RELENTLESS AND RUTHLESS, WHO HAD DISGRACED HUMANITY BY INFLICTING CRUEL OUTRAGES UPON INOFFENSIVE MEN AND WOMEN, AND EVEN UPON THE LIFELESS DEAD, WERE NOW COMPLETELY AT HIS MERCY. BUT IN THE HOUR OF HIS TRIUMPH EVERY EVIL SUFFERED WAS FORGOTTEN, EVERY INJURY INFLICTED WAS FORGIVEN, AND A GENERAL AMNESTY WAS EXTENDED TO THE POPULATION OF MAKKAH ..."
>
> *Sayed Amir Ali in **"The Spirit of Islam."***

Calling before him the populace of the vanquished city, he addressed them with **"What do you expect at my hands today?"** His people had known him too well, even from his childhood so they replied, "Mercy, O generous brother and nephew!" Tears came into the eyes of the Prophet, and he said, **"I will speak to you as Joseph spoke unto his brethren, I will not reproach you today; go you are free!"**

And now a scene was enacted of which there is really no parallel in the history of the world. Hosts upon hosts came forward and adopted the religion of Islam. God Almighty testifies as to the lofty and exalted behaviour of His Messenger —

---

1. A fulfilment of another prophecy in Muhummed (pbuh). **". . . He came from mount Paran (that is in Arabia), and he came with ten thousand saints . . ."** Deuteronomy 33:2.

Ye have indeed in the Messenger of Allah a beautiful pattern (of conduct)

Holy Qur'an 33:21

How well has Lamartine[1] unknowingly echoed these sentiments —

"AS REGARDS **ALL STANDARDS** BY WHICH HUMAN GREATNESS MAY BE MEASURED, WE MAY WELL ASK, IS THERE ANY MAN GREATER THAN HE?"

In reply, we too can say once more, **"No! there is no man greater than Muhummed (pbuh). Muhummed (pbuh) was the greatest man that ever lived!"**

So far, our hero has earned the unsolicited and ungrudging tributes from many non-Muslims of different religious persuasions and from varying intellectual fields of endeavour. But all this still remains incomplete without the Master's verdict; Muhummed's (pbuh) predecessor — Jesus Christ (pbuh). We will now apply his own standard for evaluating greatness.

JOHN THE BAPTIST

John the Baptist,[2] known throughout the Muslim world as Hazrat ***Yahya*** Alaihis-salaam (Peace be upon him) was, a contemporary prophet of the Messiah. They were also cousins. Here is what the Master has to say of him:

---

1. Full quotation of Larmartine will be found in Appendix "B" on page 61.
2. "JOHN" not to be confused with John the disciple of Jesus (pbuh). A very common name among the Jews and Arabs, even today, like Tarik Aziz the current Iraqi Minister of Foreign Affairs. Real name Tarik **Hanna** Aziz; **"Hanna"** short for Yuhanna meaning John. No one in the non-Arab Muslim world knowing that our friend is a Christian Marxist.

> *Verily I say unto you, Among them that are born of women there hath not risen a greater than John the Baptist:*
>
> Matthew 11:11

Every son of man is **"born of women."** By this very fact John the Baptist is greater than Moses, David, Solomon, Abraham or Isaiah; none of the Israelite prophets excluded. What gives John this ascendency over every other prophet? It could not be any miracle, because the Bible records none to his credit. It could not be his teachings, because he brought no new laws or regulations. Then what makes him the greatest? Simply because he was the heralder, a precursor, a harbinger of the happy news of the coming of the Messiah. This is what made John the greatest, but Jesus (pbuh) claims that he himself was even greater than the greatest (ie. John). Why?

> *But I have greater witness than that of John* (the Baptist): *For The Works which the Father hath given me to finish:* (Emphasis added)
>
> John 5:36

It is the **"witness,"** the commission which God Almighty had entrusted him with, which makes Jesus (pbuh) greater than even John. Applying these very standards as enunciated by the Master, we find that —

1. John the Baptist was the greatest of all the Israelite prophets, because he heralded the mighty Messiah (Jesus pbuh).

   Similarly Jesus (pbuh) would be greater than even John because he heralded **"The Spirit of**

Truth, the Comforter," who was to guide mankind into **all Truth** (of the Gospel of St. John, chapter 16).[1]

2. The diocese, the mission of Jesus (pbuh), or **"the works which God had given him to accomplish,"** was limited to the Lost sheep of the House of Israel (Matthew 15:24), whereas the mission of Muhummed (pbuh) was universal. He had been told —

> *And we have sent thee not (O Muhummed), but as a Mercy unto (all) the worlds.*
>
> Holy Qur'an 21:107

In keeping with his grand commission, Muhummed (pbuh) consistently delivered his Message to one and all who would hear, irrespective of race, class or creed, He welcomed them all in the religion of God, without any discrimination. He had no thought of dividing the creatures of God into **"dogs and pigs"** (Matthew 7:6) or into **"sheep and goats"** (Matthew 25:32). He was the Messenger of the One True God, who was sent as a Mercy unto all mankind, nay, unto the whole universe (H.Q. 21:107 above). And, he never forgot this mission even right up to his dying day.

Towards the end of his earthly sojourn, when he could look back to a hectic and dangerous past, now crowned with success; he now feels that he could sit back and enjoy the fruits of his toil; he dreams of a life free from turmoil and full of satisfaction and relaxation. Not for him! There is no time to rest or relax. There is work still to be done. God Almighty reminds him — —

---

1. For a detailed explanation about this prophecy, obtain today your FREE copy of the book **"MUHUMMED (pbuh) the Natural Successor to CHRIST (pbuh)"** from the IPCI.

WE HAVE NOT SENT THEE** (O MUHUMMED) **BUT TO THE WHOLE OF MANKIND,

وَمَآ أَرْسَلْنَٰكَ إِلَّا كَآفَّةً لِّلنَّاسِ

AS A GIVER OF GLAD TIDINGS AND AS A WARNER,

بَشِيرًا وَنَذِيرًا

BUT MOST OF MANKIND STILL DO NOT KNOW.

وَلَٰكِنَّ أَكْثَرَ ٱلنَّاسِ لَا يَعْلَمُونَ ۝

Holy Qur'an 34:28 [1]

How was he to respond to this new challenge in his ripening old age? There were no electronic gadgets of modern communication methods at his disposal; there were no telex and fax machines which he could exploit. What could he do? Being an **ummi** (unlettered), he called the scribes and dictated five letters, one each to the Emperor at Constantinople, the King of Egypt, the Negus of Abyssinia, the King of Yemen and to the Emperor in Persia. He called forth five ***Sahaaba*** (his holy companions) with five Arab steeds and set them out in five different directions inviting the nations of the world to the universal religion of God.

I had the good fortune of seeing one of those holy epistles in the Topkapi Museum in Istanbul (old Constantinople) Turkey. That letter is collecting dust! Materially the Turks have preserved the parchment. But the Message is collecting dust, as I have said.

The letter begins, **"From Muhummed the Messenger of God, to Heraclius the Emperor at Constantinople: Accept Islam and be benefited."**

Followed by this exhortation from the Book of God — —

---

1. This is your last chance to memorize the text and the translation of this verse. If you are lackadaisical, we can only mourn your loss.

SAY: "O PEOPLE OF THE BOOK! [1] — قُلْ يٰٓاَهْلَ الْكِتٰبِ

COME TO COMMON TERMS AS BETWEEN US AND YOU: — تَعَالَوْا اِلٰى كَلِمَةٍ سَوَآءٍۭ بَيْنَنَا وَبَيْنَكُمْ

THAT WE WORSHIP NONE BUT GOD; — اَلَّا نَعْبُدَ اِلَّا اللّٰهَ

THAT WE ASSOCIATE NO PARTNERS WITH HIM; — وَلَا نُشْرِكَ بِهٖ شَيْـًٔا

THAT WE ERECT NOT, FROM AMONG OURSELVES, LORDS AND PATRONS OTHER THAN GOD." — وَّلَا يَتَّخِذَ بَعْضُنَا بَعْضًا اَرْبَابًا مِّنْ دُوْنِ اللّٰهِ

IF THEN THEY TURN BACK, SAY YE: "BEAR WITNESS THAT WE (AT LEAST) ARE MUSLIMS (BOWING TO GOD'S WILL)" — فَاِنْ تَوَلَّوْا فَقُوْلُوا اشْهَدُوْا بِاَنَّا مُسْلِمُوْنَ ○

Holy Qur'an 3:64

After the above Qur'anic insertion in the letter, it is concluded with felicitation in the Prophet's own words, ending with a seal on which is inscribed — **"There is no other object of worship but Allah, and Muhummed is His Messenger."**

The letter in Turkey arouses our curiosity; and interest with regards to its preservation, but the preservation itself is lost upon the sightseer. The same Qur'anic Message is in almost every Muslim home; being read and re-read a thousand times over without the reader being moved to deliver its Message to the addressees!

Glance once more at the above verse. It is addressed to the **"ahle-Kitaab,"** — the People of the Book, the Jews and

---

1. **"People of the Book,"** stands for the Jews and the Christians. You will never have it so good for learning Allah's ***Kalaam***. Don't ignore this opportunity. Memorize the verses as they occur

the Christians. But, for over a thousand years we have utterly ignored that great directive at our own peril. We are sitting on that Message like a cobra on a pile of wealth, keeping the rightful heirs at bay. This utter neglect will continue to inflict untold suffering to the **Ummah** for generations to come.

After over fourteen hundred years of our reading, and chanting the Qur'an in every rhythmic style, we still hear this poignant cry:

> ***But Most of mankind still do not know.***[1]
>
> Holy Qur'an 34:28

This is the concluding phrase of the verse revealed fourteen hundred years ago. It was the factual situation of the then religious world. The question which must be asked is it any different today? **Not at all!** There are today more ***Mushriks*** in the world than there are believers in the One True God.

Is there any hope of changing this situation? Allah commanded His Prophet then as He is commanding us now through the first seven verses of Sura ***Muddaththir*** (chapter 74).

1. ***O THOU WRAPPED UP (IN A MANTLE)!*** يَاأَيُّهَا الْمُدَّثِّرُ ۝

"As usual, there is these wonderful early mystical verses (including the ones that follow), a triple thread of thought:

(a) A particular occasion or person is referred to;

---

1. For the full context of this verse, see page 54.

(b) a general spiritual lesson is taught, and

(c) a more profound mystical reverie is suggested.

As to (a), the Prophet was now past the stage of personal contemplation. Wearing his mantle; he was now to go forth and boldly deliver his Message and publicly proclaim Allah The One True God. His heart had always been purified, but now all his outward doings must be dedicated to God, and conventional respect for ancestral customs or worship must be thrown aside. The work of his Messengership was the most generous that could flow from his personality, but no reward or appreciation was to be expected from his people, but quite the contrary; there would be much call on his patience, but his contentment would arise from the good pleasure of God.

As to (b), similar stages arise in a minor degree in the life of every good man, for which the Prophet's life is to be a universal pattern.

As to (c), the ***Sufis*** understand, by the mantle and outward wrappings, the circumstances of our phenomenal existence, which are necessary to our physical comfort up to a certain stage; but we soon outgrow them, and our inner nature should then boldly proclaim itself; not that it brings any credit or reward with men; the very hope of expectation of such would be inconsistent with our higher nature, which should bear all checks and rejoice in the favour of God."

2. ***ARISE AND DELIVER THY WARNING!*** قُمْ فَأَنذِرْ ۝

3. ***AND THY LORD DO THOU MAGNIFY!*** وَرَبَّكَ فَكَبِّرْ ۝

4. ***AND THY GARMENTS KEEP FREE FROM STAIN!*** وَثِيَابَكَ فَطَهِّرْ ۝

5. ***AND ALL ABOMINATION SHUN!*** (a) وَالرُّجْزَ فَاهْجُرْ ۝

"**(a) Rujz** or **Rijz** means abomination and is usually understood to mean idolatry. It is even possible that there was an idol called **Rujz.** But these days it has a wider significance as including a mental state opposed to true worship, a state of doubt or indecision."

6. ***NOR EXPECT, IN GIVING, ANY INCREASE (FOR THYSELF)!*** (b) وَلَا تَمْنُنْ تَسْتَكْثِرُ ۝

"**(b)** The legal and commercial formula is that you give in order to receive what is worth **to you** a little more than you give, but expect nothing from the receiver. You serve God and God's creatures."

7. ***BUT, FOR THY LORD'S (CAUSE) BE PATIENT AND CONSTANT!*** (c)[1] وَلِرَبِّكَ فَاصْبِرْ ۝

Holy Qur'an 74:1—7

"**(c)** Our zeal for God's Cause itself requires that we should not be impatient, and that we should show constancy in our efforts for His Cause. For we have faith, and we know that He is All-Good, All-Wise, and All-Powerful, and everything will ultimately be right."

Abdullah Yusuf Ali[2]

---

1. **Remember** to memorize Allah's ***Kalaam*** with its meaning!

2. **The** English translation and the commentaries was by Abdullah Yusuf Ali. Obtain your **volume** from the IPCI at a specially subsidised price. **Also order a volume for your non-Muslim friend.**

To the Arabs in general and to our Holy Prophet in particular **"a mantle"** was the protective covering used for protection against the sun, wind and sand. He was so to say girding himself, rolling up his sleeves, to accomplish his task. Although most of the Muslims in the world do not cover themselves with shawls (mantles), in their day to day living, they carry a host of mantles in the way of inferiority complexes.

WHAT CAN WE DO TO MAKE GOD'S LIGHT
SHINE FORTH THROUGH THE DARKNESS AROUND US?
WE MUST FIRST LET IT SHINE IN OUR OWN TRUE SELVES
WITH THAT LIGHT IN THE NICHE OF OUR INMOST HEARTS
WE CAN WALK WITH STEPS BOTH FIRM AND SURE:
WE CAN HUMBLY VISIT THE COMFORTLESS
AND GUIDE THEIR STEPS. NOT WE, BUT THE LIGHT
WILL GUIDE! BUT OH! THE JOY OF BEING FOUND
WORTHY TO BEAR THE TORCH, AND TO SAY
TO OUR BRETHREN: "I TOO WAS IN DARKNESS,
COMFORTLESS, AND BEHOLD, I HAVE FOUND
COMFORT AND JOY IN THE GRACE DIVINE!"
THUS SHOULD WE PAY THE DUES OF BROTHERHOOD, — —
BY WALKING HUMBLY SIDE BY SIDE,
IN THE WAYS OF THE LORD,
WITH MUTUAL AID AND COMFORT,
AND HEARTFELT PRAYER,
BACKED BY ACTION,
THAT GOD'S GOOD PURPOSE
MAY BE ACCOMPLISHED
IN US ALL TOGETHER!

Abdullah Yusuf Ali

وَلٰكِنَّ اَكْثَرَ النَّاسِ لَا يَعْلَمُوْنَ ○

BUT MOST OF MANKIND
STILL DO NOT KNOW

Thus spake, inspired our Holy Prophet, Muhummed (pbuh) on whom we invoke God's blessings for ever and ever –

AAMEEN!

Ahmed Deedat
25/11/90

APPENDIX "A"

بَلَغَ الْعُلیٰ بِکَمَالِہٖ

He attained the height of eminence by his perfection;

کَشَفَ الدُّجیٰ بِجَمَالِہٖ

He dispelled the darkness (of the world) by his grace;

حَسُنَتْ جَمِیْعُ خِصَالِہٖ

Excellent were all his qualities;

صَلُّوْا عَلَیْہِ وَاٰلِہٖ

Pray for blessings on him and his descendants.

Shaikh Sa'di Sheeraazi (RA)

APPENDIX "B"

Muhummed (PBUH) The Greatest

"If greatness of purpose,
smallness of means
and astounding results

are the three criteria of human genius, who could dare to compare any great man in modern history with Muhummed?

The most famous men created arms, laws and empires only. They founded, if anything at all, no more than material powers which often crumbled away before their eyes. This man Muhammed moved not only armies, legislations, empires, peoples and dynasties, but millions of men; and more than that the altars, the gods, the religions, the ideas, the beliefs and the souls.

On the basis of a Book, every letter of which has become law, he created a spiritual nationality which blended together peoples of every tongue and of every race . . .

The idea of the unity of God, proclaimed amidst the exhaustion of fabulous theologies, was in itself such a miracle that upon its utterance from his lips it destroyed all the ancient superstitions . . .

His endless prayers, his mystic conversations with God, his death and his triumph after death: all these attest not to an imposture but to a firm conviction which gave him the power to restore a dogma. This dogma was twofold, **the unity of God and the immateriality of God;** the former telling what God is, the latter telling what God is not . . .

. . . "PHILOSOPHER, ORATOR, APOSTLE, LEGISLATOR, WARRIOR, CONQUEROR OF IDEAS, RESTORER OF RATIONAL BELIEFS, of a cult without images; the founder of twenty terrestrial empires and of one spiritual empire, that is Muhammed. **AS REGARDS ALL STANDARDS BY WHICH HUMAN GREATNESS MAY BE MEASURED, WE MAY WELL ASK, IS THERE ANY MAN GREATER THAN HE?"**

(Lamartine, Historie de la Turquie, Paris 1854, Vol II pp.276-277).

APPENDIX "C"

JULES MASSERMAN, U.S. psychoanalyst:

TIME, JULY 15, 1974

Leaders must fulfil three functions — — — provide for the well-being of the led, provide a social organization in which people feel relatively secure, and provide them with one set of beliefs. People like Pasteur and Salk are leaders in the first sense.

People like Gandhi and Confucius, on one hand, and Alexander, Caesar and Hitler on the other, are leaders in the second and perhaps the third sense. Jesus and Buddha belong in the third category alone. **PERHAPS THE GREATEST LEADER OF ALL TIMES WAS MOHAMMED, WHO COMBINED ALL THREE FUNCTIONS.** To a lesser degree Moses did the same. (Emphasis added)

APPENDIX "D"

Fidelity is said to be a human attribute,

Which makes the modern gentleman distinguished from the brute,

But that supreme fidelity, inborn in every hound,

Which is the mark of man's best friend,

In man, it's rarely found!

A South African Poet.

APPENDIX 'C'

TIME MAGAZINE, U.S.A. [illegible]
DATE: JULY 15, 1974

Leaders must fulfil three functions — provide for the well-being of the led, provide a social organisation in which people feel relatively secure, and provide them with one set of beliefs. People like Pasteur and Salk are leaders in the first sense.

People like Gandhi and Confucius, on one hand, and Alexander, Caesar and Hitler on the other, are leaders in the second and perhaps the third sense. Jesus and Buddha belong in the third category alone. PERHAPS THE GREATEST LEADER OF ALL TIMES WAS MOHAMMAD, WHO COMBINED ALL THREE FUNCTIONS. To a lesser degree, Moses did the same. (Emphasis added)

APPENDIX 'D'

[illegible] is said to be a human [illegible]

Which makes the [illegible] distinguished from a brute

But that [illegible]

Which [illegible] of [illegible]

[illegible]

— [illegible]